FREE STYLE SCRAPS ⓪⓵
SILHOUETTE

Copyright © 2006 4D2A

Published by   BNN, Inc.
                      11F Shinjuku Square Tower Building
                      6-22-1 Nishishinjuku Shinjuku-ku
                      Tokyo 163-1111
                      Mail: info@bnn.co.jp

Edited & Designed by 4D2A

Illustrated by   Ryo Arai
                      Hisashi Okawa
                      Mio Oguma
                      Satoshi Sakagami(METEOR)
                      Yusuke Shouno
                      Hiroki Tsukuda
                      Kurando Furuya
                      Shinpei Yamamori

Translated by   R.I.C. Publication Asia Co., Inc.

ISBN 4-86100-412-8

Printed in Japan by Shinano, Ltd.

FREE STYLE SCRAPS 01 SILHOUETTE　ライセンス契約書

1. ライセンス

1) 株式会社ビー・エヌ・エヌ新社 (以下「弊社」という。) は、本製品を購入され、本ライセンス契約書記載の条件に合意されたお客様 (以下「ユーザー」という。) に対し、本ソフトウェアを同時に 1 台のコンピュータ上でのみ使用できる、譲渡不能の非独占的権利を許諾します。

2) ユーザーは、2 の「制限事由」に該当する場合を除き、本ソフトウェアに含まれる素材を加工・編集し、もしくは他の素材と組み合わせるなどして、主に以下のデザインに使用することができます。

○ WEB などのデジタルメディア ○店舗の内装、案内表示などのグラフィックツール ○印刷物として頒布するチラシ、フライヤー、ポスター、DM、カタログ、パンフレットなどの広告・販売促進ツール ○個人制作・個人利用の雑貨、服、グリーティングカード、名刺など

(個人的・職業的・商業的用途の利用を認めますが、いずれも非売品のデザインに限ります。個人においても素材を利用した制作物の販売は行えません。また、書籍や雑誌など売品の印刷メディアに素材を利用する場合は、使用の範囲によって別途料金が発生する場合があります。右記連絡先までお問い合わせください。MAIL : info@4d2a.com / TEL : 03-3770-2807 / FAX : 03-3770-2807)

次の制限事由をよくお読み下さい。

2. 制限事由

以下の行為を禁止します。

1) 本ソフトウェアを 1 台のコンピュータで使用する為のやむを得ぬ場合を除き、本ソフトウェアを複製すること

2) 本ライセンス契約書に基づくライセンスを他に譲渡し、本製品の貸与もしくはその他の方法で本ソフトウェアを他者に使用させること

3) 流通を目的とした商品のデザインに素材を利用すること

4) 著作権者に無断で、書籍や雑誌など売品の印刷メディアに素材を利用すること

5) 素材を利用してポストカード、名刺、雑貨などの制作販売または制作サービスを行うこと

6) 素材を利用してインターネットによるダウンロードサービスを行うこと (グリーティングカード・サービスを含む)

7) 素材をホームページ上で公開する場合に、オリジナルデータがダウンロード可能となる環境を作ること

8) ソフトウェア製品等を製造・販売するために素材を流用すること

9) 素材そのものや素材を用いた制作物について意匠権などの権利を取得すること

10) 素材を公序良俗に反する目的、誹謗・中傷目的で利用すること

3. 著作権、その他の知的財産権

本ソフトウェアおよび素材に関する著作権、その他の知的財産権は、弊社または弊社への供給者の排他的財産として留保されています。素材を利用した制作物においてユーザーの著作権を明示する場合は、素材の著作権「©4D2A」を併記してください。

4. 責任の制限

弊社および弊社への供給者は、請求原因の如何を問わず、本ソフトウェアの使用または使用の不能および素材の利用から生じるすべての損害や不利益 (利益の逸失およびデータの損壊を含む。) につき、一切責任を負わないものとします。

5. 使用許諾の終了

ユーザーが本ライセンス契約書に違反した場合、弊社は、本ライセンス契約書に基づくユーザーのライセンスを終了させることができます。

FREE STYLE SCRAPS ⓪①SILHOUETTE   License Agreement of the Software

1. License

1) This License Agreement is a legal agreement between you (the "User"), who purchased the product Petit Pattern Book: Flowers & Leaves, and BNN, Inc. ("BNN"), in respect of the attached CD-ROM entitled Petit Pattern Book: Flowers & Leaves ("Software"). The User agrees to be bound by the terms of this License Agreement by installing, copying, or using the Software. BNN grants the User the right to use a copy of the Software on one personal computer for the exclusive use of the User.

2) The User may modify, edit, or combine the materials included in the Software except the cases specified in "2. Limitations"; the User has the right to use the Software principally for design of the following objects.

○ Digital media including websites.

○ Graphics for shop interiors, signs, etc.

○ Leaflets, flyers, posters, direct mail, catalogues, pamphlets, and other tools for advertisement or sales promotion.

○ Goods, clothes, greeting cards, name cards and other articles for personal production and use.

 (The Software may be used for personal, professional, and commercial purposes, provided that the articles produced are not offered for sale. If the software is used to design products for distribution including books and magazines, a copyright fee may occur according to the scale of use. You must contact the copyright holder. e-mail : info@4d2a.com / TEL : 03-3770-2807 / FAX : 03-3770-2807)

Please read the following Limitations carefully.

2. Limitations

The User is not licensed to do any of the following:

1) Copy the Software, unless copying it is unavoidable to enable it to be used on one personal computer.

2) License, or otherwise by any means permit, any other person to use the Software.

3) Use the Software to design of products for distribution.

4) Design of products for distribution including books and magazines.

5) Use the Software for the commercial production of postcards, name cards, or any other articles, or sell any such articles made using the Software.

6) Provide downloading services using the Software (including greeting card services).

7) Create an environment which allows the original data to be downloaded when you show one of the Software patterns on a home page.

8) Use the Software in order to produce any software or other products for sale.

9) Acquire the copyright in any material in the Software or any object you have created using the Software.

10) Use the Software to create obscene, scandalous, abusive or slanderous works.

3. Copyright and other intellectual property

BNN or its suppliers reserves the copyright and other intellectual property rights in the Software. When specifying the User's copyright of a product made using the Software, please also write "©4D2A".

4. Exclusion of damages

In no event shall BNN be liable for any damages whatsoever (including but not limited to, damages for loss of profit or loss of data) related to the use or inability to use of the Software or use of materials in the Software.

5. Termination of this License Agreement

If the User breaches this License Agreement, BNN has the right to withdraw the User's License granted on the basis hereof.

CD-ROM をご使用になる前に

○注意すること
● 必ず P.002 のライセンス契約書をお読みください。
● Mac OS X (10.4.5)、Adobe Photoshop CS2、Adobe Illustrator CS2、Windows XP で動作確認済みですが、環境が異なる場合や、操作方法が分からないときは、OS やソフトウェアに則した、お手持ちの説明書をお読みください。

○準備
まずは CD-ROM をセットして、「FSS_01」フォルダを開きます。必要なデータをピックアップし、デスクトップにコピーしましょう。「FSS_01」フォルダには「JPEG」と「EPS」という 2 つのフォルダが入っています。

○データの種類
掲載したすべてのイラストレーションは、それぞれ JPEG と EPS の 2 つの形式でファイルを用意しています。（データーはすべてモノクロになっています。EPS ファイルは、Illustrator のバージョン 8.0 で保存しています。）

JPEG
JPEG ファイルとして収録したのは、350dpi（商業印刷に耐え得る解像度）に設定したときに、掲載サイズと等倍の印刷面積を持つビットマップ画像。「Adobe Photoshop」をはじめとするビットマップ系のソフトウェアで編集できるほか、多くのソフトウェアで扱うことが可能です。

EPS
EPS ファイルとして収録したのは、拡大縮小を行っても画質が劣化しない、ベクトル画像。ドロー系のソフトウェア「Adobe Illustrator」でファイルを開くと、自由にカスタマイズできます。（ビットマップ系のソフトウェア「Adobe Photoshop」で開くと、「ラスタライズ」という工程を経て、ビットマップイメージに展開します。）

○データの見つけ方
JPEG データはイラストレーション 1 点につき 1 ファイルとなっていて、下の図のように、ページごとにナンバリングされています。（たとえば 234 ページの場合「p234_01.jpg」「p234_02.jpg」「p234_03.jpg」「p234_04.jpg」「p234_05.jpg」「p234_06.jpg」「p234_07.jpg」、235 ページの場合「p235_01.jpg」「p235_02.jpg」「p235_03.jpg」「p235_04.jpg」「p235_05.jpg」「p235_06.jpg」というファイル名で収録されています。）EPS データは見開き単位で 1 ファイルとなっています。（たとえば 234 ページと 235 ページの見開きの場合「p234_235.eps」というファイル名で収録されます。）

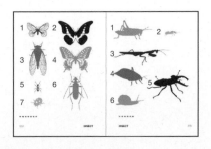

Before you start using the CD-ROM

○ Notes

● Please read the conditions of use on page 002.

● The functionality has been verified with Mac OS X (10.4.5), Adobe Photoshop CS2, Adobe Illustrator CS2, and Windows XP Professional SP1. If your system is different, or if you have a question concerning the operation of the software, refer to the manuals corresponding to your OS and software.

○ Preparation

Set the CD-ROM and open the folder "FSS_01". Copy the folders you need onto your desktop. There are two folders in "FSS_01": "JPEG" and "EPS".

○ Different kinds of data

All the illustration in the book are prepared in the following two formats:
(EPS files are saved with Illustrator 8.0.)

※ In the JPEG file, you will find bitmap images which are printed on the same size as shown in the book at 350 dpi (the resolution suitable for commercial printing). You can edit them with Adobe Photoshop and other bitmap software, and you can use it with many other types of software.

※ In the EPS file, you will find vector images, which do not deteriorate when you increase or reduce the size. Open the file with Adobe Illustrator or other drawing software, and you will be able to customize the images freely. (When you open the file with bitmap software such as Adobe Photoshop, the image will be developed as a bitmap image after the process called rasterizing).

○ How to find the data

As for the JPEG data, there is a separate file for each illustration. The illustrations in each page are numbered from top left as shown below. For example, the illustrations on page 234 are named "p234_01.jpg", "p234_02.jpg", "p234_03.jpg", "p234_04.jpg", "p234_05.jpg", "p234_06.jpg", "p234_07.jpg"; as for page 235, "p235_01.jpg", "p235_02.jpg", "p235_03.jpg", "p235_04.jpg", "p235_05.jpg", "p235_06.jpg".
As for the EPS data, there is a file for two facing pages. For example, all the illustrations on pages 234 and 235 are found in the file "p234_235.eps".

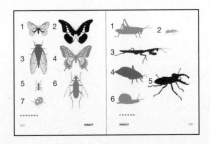

EXAMPLE

いつでもどこでもデザインやレイアウトがしたい。
これは、そんなあなたのための素材集です。プレゼンテーションやウェブ制作の現場、ビジ
ネス、また生活のさまざまな場面で役立つよう、幅広いテーマから素材を選び、それぞれ1000
点以上のイラストレーションを収録しています。また、誰でも簡単に利用できるよう、掲載し
たイラストレーションのすべてを、付属する CD-ROM に汎用性の高い JPEG 形式と、Adobe
Illustrator のベジェデータとして扱える EPS 形式で収録しています。

「マグカップ」帯状に花のシルエットをあしらいました。
1 個からも注文できる専門業者に発注。「CD」コート紙
に 4 色印刷。
※上記の作例はすべてオンライン入稿。ネットで検索し
た業者によって 1 週間程度で制作。

"Mugs" designed with horizontal flower patterns, can
be placed to specialized manufacturers."CD jackets"
can be printed in four colors on coated paper.
※ We placed the orders of all the examples above to
manufacturers which we found on the internet. We
received the goods a week later.

This book is for you who wants to design anytime, anywhere. It provides efficient, simple, versatile and accessible design materials for you. The materials are categorized by wide range of subjects suitable for multiple-purposes such as presentations, website designs, hobbies etc. There are more than 1000 illustrations per subject. Moreover all the illustrations included can be used as JPEG files or EPS files with bezier curves for Adobe Illustrator in the CD-ROM.

「ステッカー」専門業者に委託。「バッヂ」小ロット対応
のバッヂ業者に委託。
※上記の作例はすべてオンライン入稿。ネットで検索し
た業者によって１週間程度で制作。

"Stickers" can be ordered from specialized manufacturers."Badges" can be ordered from specialized manufacturers.
※ We placed the orders of all the examples above to manufacturers which we found on the internet. We received the goods a week later.

FREE STYLE SCRAPS 01
SILHOUETTE

01 02 03

CITY

CITY

01 02 03 04 05 06

HOUSE

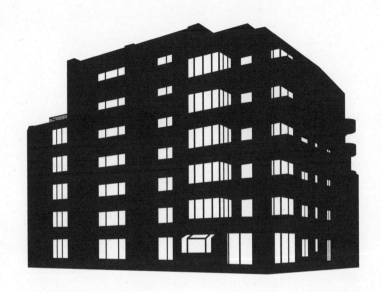

01 02 03

HOUSE

01 02 03

CASTLE

01 02 03 04

CASTLE 015

PARK

BUS STOP

01 02 03

BUS STOP

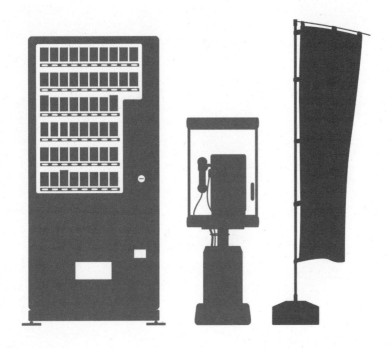

VENDING MACHINE

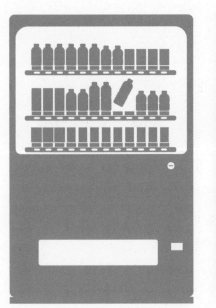
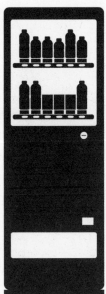

01 02 03

VENDING MACHINE 021

01 02 03 04 05

GARBAGE

01 02 03

GARBAGE

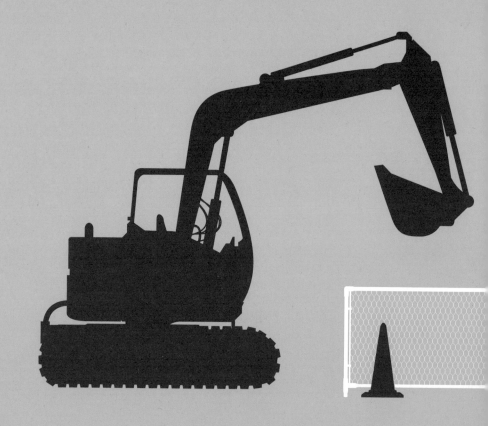

CONSTRUCTION

CONSTRUCTION

POLICE

01 02 03 04

POLICE

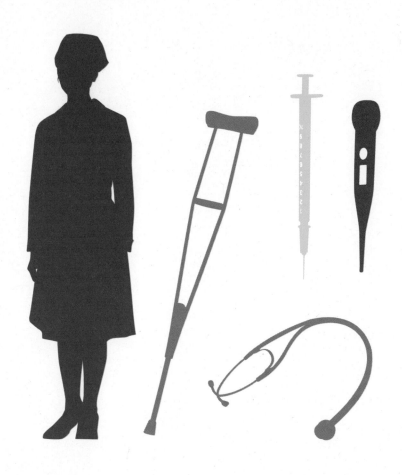

01 02 03 04 05

HOSPITAL

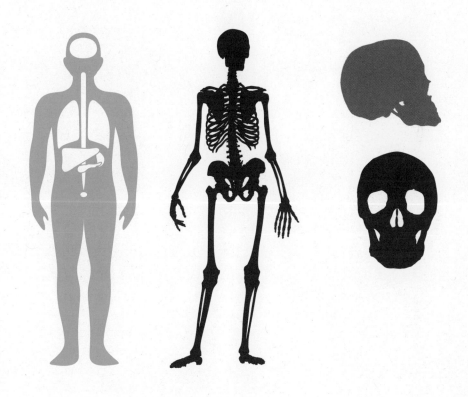

01 02 03 04

SKELETON

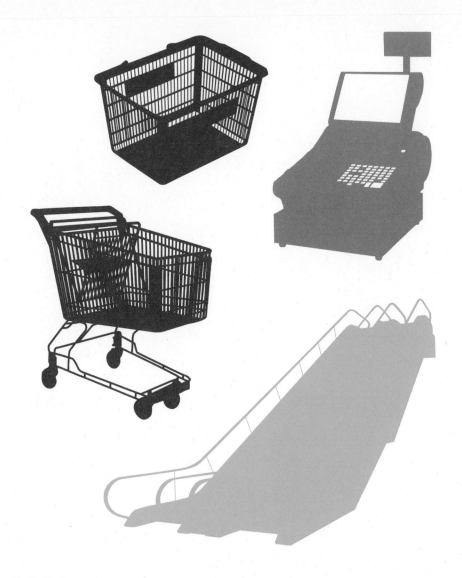

01 02 03 04

TRAIN

01 02

CABLE CAR

01 02

SHIP   035

01 02 03 04 05

CAR

01 02 03 04 05

CAR 037

01 02 03

SCRAPER 039

01 02 03 04 05

MOTORCYCLE

01 02 03 04 05

MOTORCYCLE

01 02 03

BICYCLE

01 02 03 04

BICYCLE

01 02 03 04

BICYCLE

01 02 03 04 05 06

SKATE

01 02 03 04 05 06

DANCE

01 02 03 04

01 02 03 04 05 06

SPORTS

01 02 03 04 05 06

01 02 03 04

SPORTS

01 02

SPORTS

01 02

SPORTS

01 02 03 04

058

BALLET DANCER

01 02 03 04

YOGA

01 02 03 04

EXERCISE

01 02 03 04

JUDO & KARATE

01 02 03 04

MARINE

01 02 03 04

SKY

01 02 03 04 05 06

CLIMBING

01 02 03 04

RAIN

WALKING

STROLL OF DOG

SITTING

01 02 03 04 05 06

SITTING

01 02 03 04 05

SITTING

01 02 03 04

SITTING

01 02 03 04 05 06

MAN

01 02 03 04 05 06

MAN

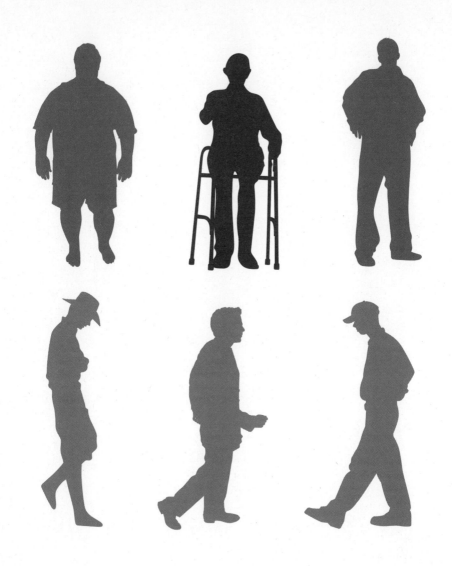

01 02 03 04 05 06

MAN

01 02 03 04 05 06

MAN   075

01 02 03 04 05 06

WOMAN

01 02 03 04 05 06

WOMAN

01 02 03 04 05 06

WOMAN

01 02 03 04 05 06

WOMAN

01 02 03 04 05 06

WOMAN

01 02 03 04 05 06

WOMAN

01 02 03 04 05 06

WOMAN

01 02 03 04 05 06

WOMAN

083

01　02　03　04　05　06

WOMAN

01 02 03 04 05 06

WOMAN

085

01 02 03 04 05 06

MARRIAGE

01 02 03 04 05 06

MARRIAGE

01 02 03 04

CEREMONY

01 02 03 04 05 06

CEREMONY

01 02 03 04

FAMILY

01   02   03   04

FAMILY

01 02 03 04 05 06 07 08

CHILD

01 02 03 04 05 06

BABY

01 02 03 04 05

BABY 095

01 02 03 04 05 06

ELDER

01　02　03　04　05

FRIENDSHIP

01 02 03 04

FELLOWSHIP

01 02

FELLOWSHIP

01 02 03 04 05 06

BUSINESSMAN

01 02 03 04 05 06

BUSINESSMAN

01 02 03 04 05

BUSINESSMAN

01 02 03 04 05 06

BUSINESSMAN

01 02 03 04 05 06

BUSINESSMAN

01 02 03 04 05

01 02 03 04

BUSINESSMAN

01 02 03 04

BUSINESSMAN

01 02 03 04 05 06

BUSINESSWOMAN

01 02 03 04 05 06

BUSINESSWOMAN

01 02 03 04

BUSINESS TALK

01 02 03 04

BUSINESS TALK

01 02 03 04 05 06

MUSICIAN

01 02 03 04 05

MUSICIAN

INSTRUMENT

01　02　03

INSTRUMENT

115

01 02 03 04 05 06

INSTRUMENT

01 02 03 04 05

INSTRUMENT 117

118 **PAINT**

01 02 03 04 05

PAINT

01 02 03 04 05 06 07 08 09

MC & DJ

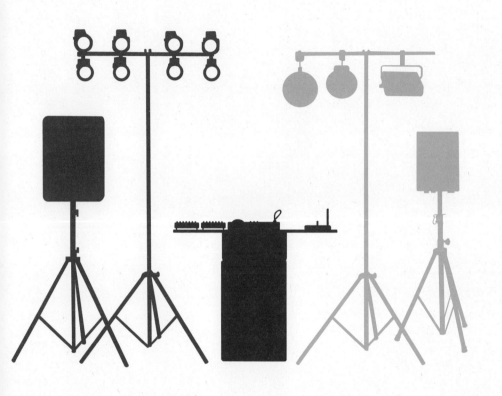

01 02 03 04 05

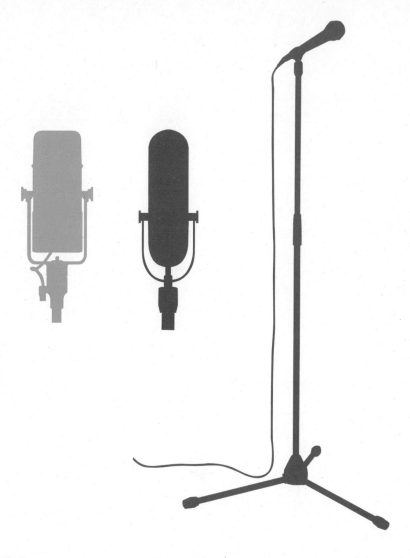

01 02 03

MICROPHONE

01 02 03

CINEMA

01 02 03

124

01 02 03 04

01 02 03

SCOPE

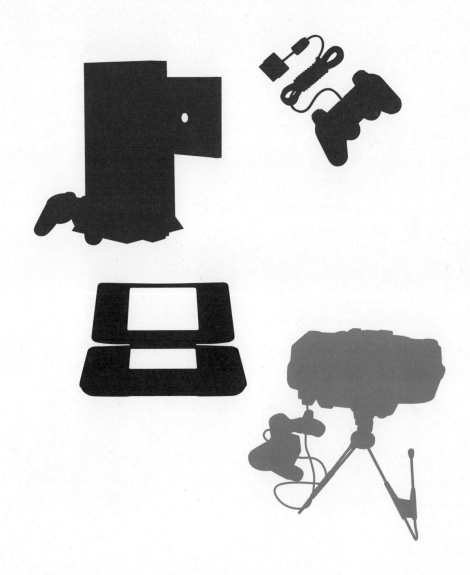

01 02 03 04

GAME

01 02 03 04 05

ROBOT

TARGET

129

01 02

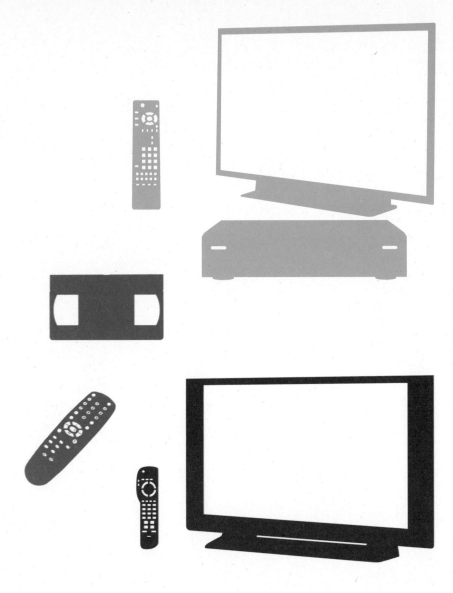

01 02 03 04

TELEVISION

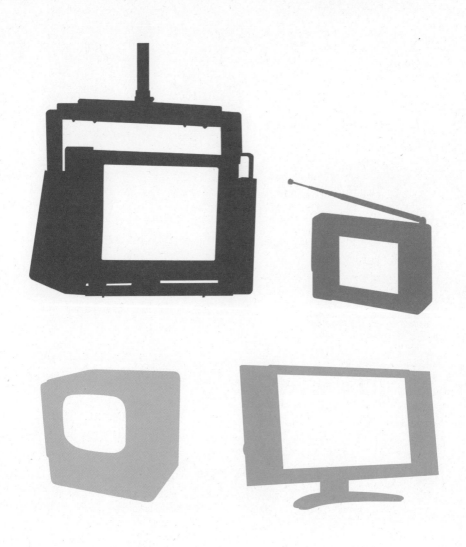

01 02 03 04

TELEVISION

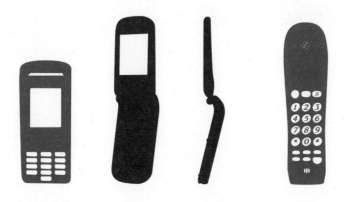

01 02 03 04 05

TELEPHONE

01 02 03

TELEPHONE

01 02 03 04 05 06

DESKTOP

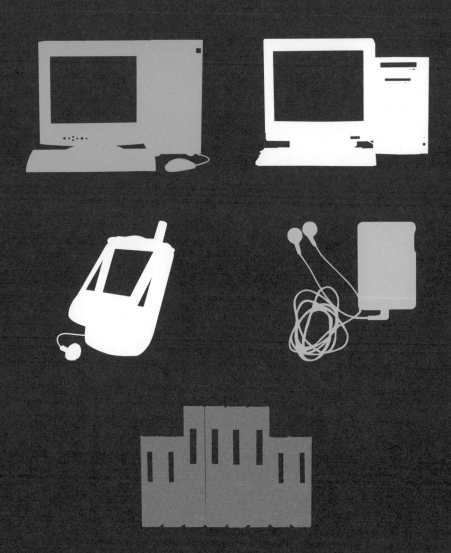

01 02 03 04 05

DESKTOP

01 02 03 04 05 06

STATIONERY

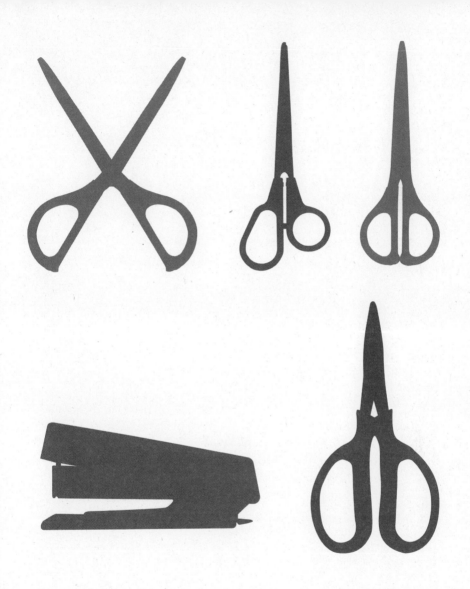

01 02 03 04 05

STATIONERY 139

01　02　03　04　05　06　07

STATIONERY

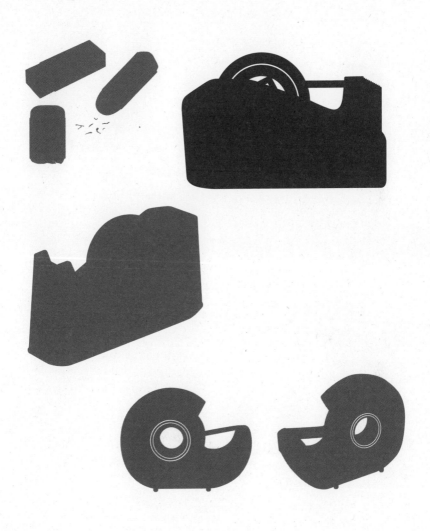

STATIONERY

01 02 03 04 05

FAN

01 02 03 04 05

CIGARETTE

01 02 03 04 05 06

LIGHT

01 02 03 04 05 06

LIGHT

LIGHT

CHANDELIER

01 02 03 04 05 06

LAMP

01 02 03 04

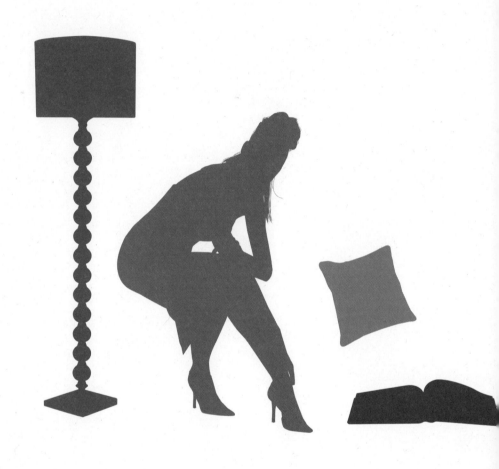

01 02 03 04

LIVING

01 02 03

SLEEP

TABLE

01 02 03 04

TABLE

01 02 03

TABLE

158   TABLE

01 02 03

CHAIR

01 02 03

CHAIR

CHAIR   161

01 02 03

162 CHAIR

01 02 03

CHAIR

01 02 03

CHAIR

01 02

CHAIR   165

01 02 03 04 05 06

CLOCK

CLOCK

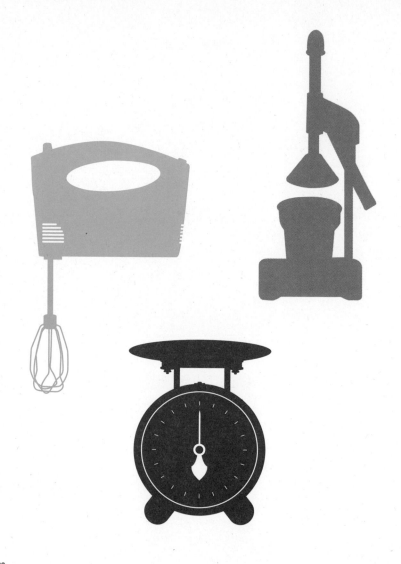

01 02 03

KITCHEN

01 02 03 04 05

01 02 03 04 05 06

170

KITCHEN

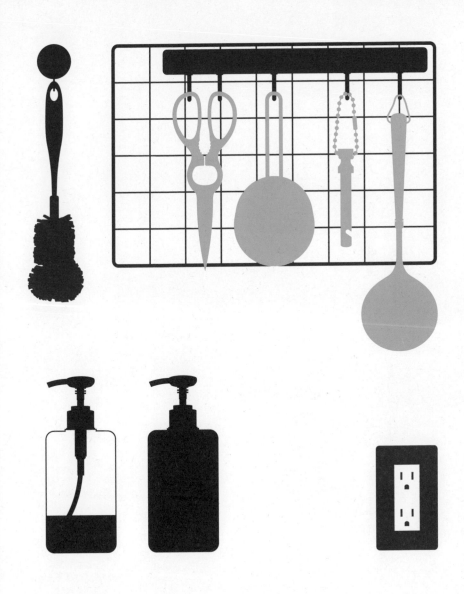

01 02 03 04 05

KITCHEN

01 02 03 04 05 06 07

KITCHEN

01 02 03 04 05 06 07

KICHEN 173

01 02 03 04 05 06 07

COFFEE

01 02 03

COFFEE

01 02 03 04 05 06 07 08

GLASS

01 02 03 04 05

01 02 03 04 05 06 07 08 09 10

GLASS & BOTTLE

01 02 03 04 05 06 07 08 09 10 11

GLASS & BOTTLE

01 02 03 04 05 06 07

FRUIT

01 02 03 04 05 06

FRUIT

01 02 03 04

SEAFOOD

01 02 03 04 05 06 07 08

VEGETABLE

Ginger
Kitchen
GINGER CHIPS

01 02 03

184   SPILL

01 02

SPILL

01 02

CLEANING

01 02 03 04

01 02 03

WASHING

01 02 03 04

01 02 03 04

BATHROOM

01 02 03 04

BATHROOM   191

01 02 03

BATHROOM

01 02 03 04 05 06

BATHROOM

01 02 03 04

WEAR

01 02 03 04 05

BAG

01 02 03 04 05 06

01 02 03 04 05 06

198

01 02 03 04 05

HAT & CAP

SHOES

SHOES

01 02 03 04 05

SHOES

01 02 03 04 05 06

SHOES

01 02 03 04

GLASSES

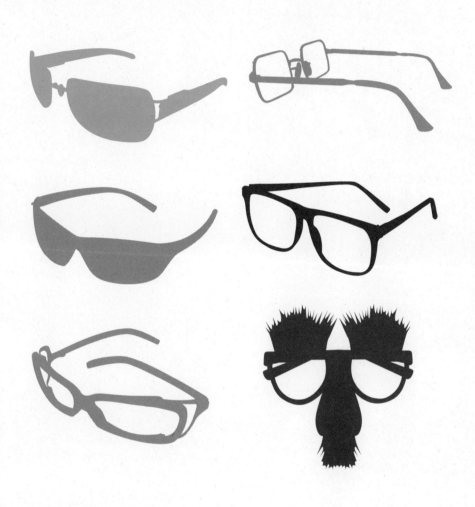

01 02 03 04 05 06

GLASSES

01 02 03 04 05 06

MASK

01 02 03 04 05

01 02 03 04 05

ACCESSORY

01 02 03 04 05 06 07

ACCESSORY

01　02　03　04　05　06

HANGER

01 02

HANGER

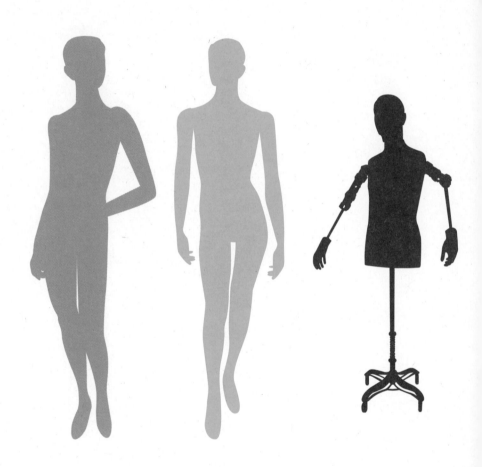

01 02 03

MANNEQUIN

01 02 03 04

MANNEQUIN

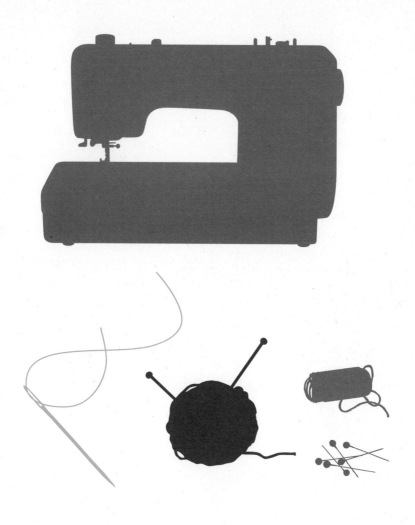

01 02 03 04 05

SEWING

01 02 03 04 05 06

MAKEUP

01 02 03

CANDLE & MIRROR

01 02 03

01 02 03 04 05 06 07 08

JAPAN

01 02

JAPAN

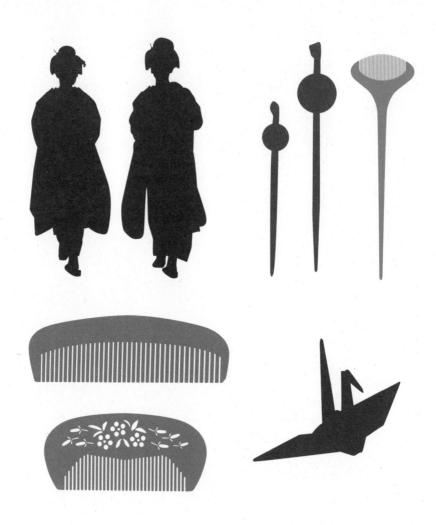

01 02 03 04 05 06 07 08

JAPAN

01 02 03

01 02 03 04 05 06 07 08 09 10

BIRD

01　02　03　04

224

ANIMAL

01 02 03 04 05

ANIMAL

01 02 03 04 05 06

ANIMAL

01 02 03

ANIMAL

01 02 03 04

ANIMAL

01 02 03 04 05 06

ANIMAL

01 02 03 04

ANIMAL

01 02 03 04

ANIMAL

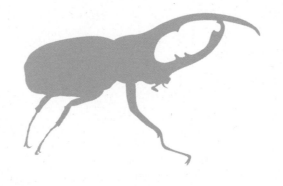

01 02 03

INSECT

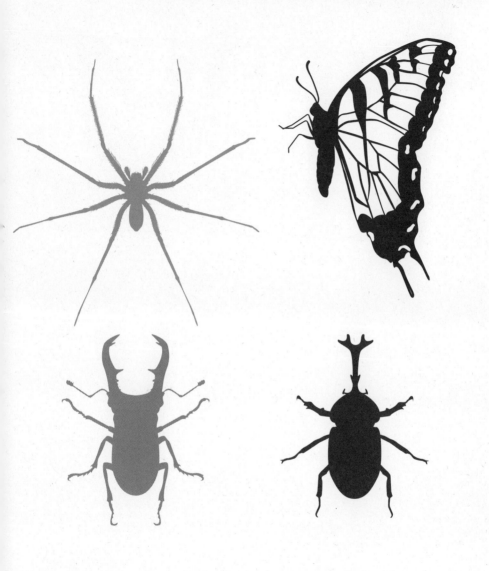

01 02 03 04

INSECT

01　02　03　04　05　06　07

INSECT

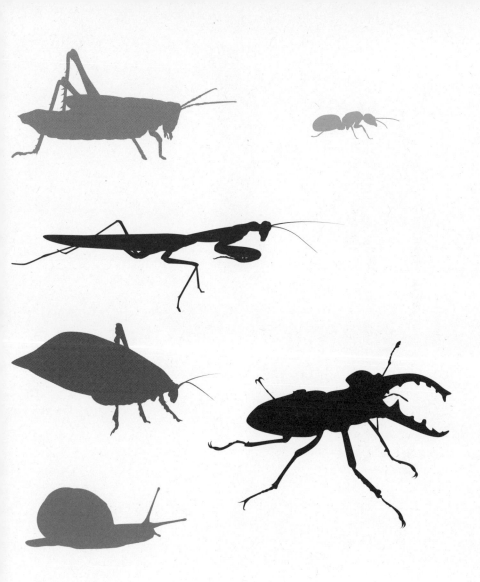

01 02 03 04 05 06

INSECT 235

01 02 03 04 05 06

WEEDING

01 02 03

CARRYING 237

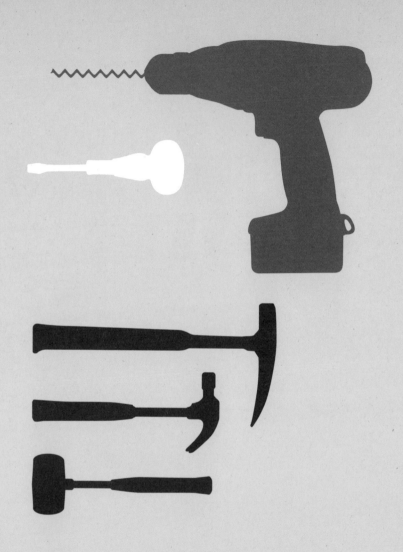

01 02 03 04 05

TOOL

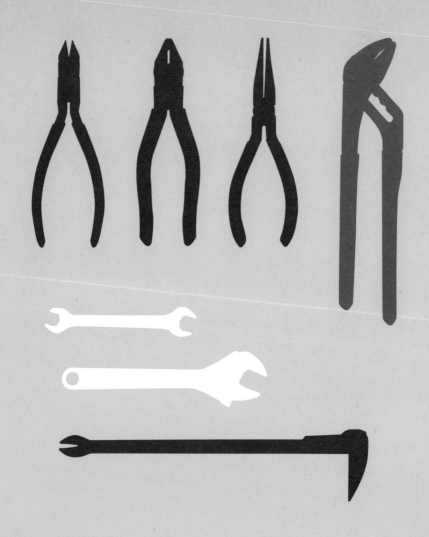

01 02 03 04 05 06 07

TOOL

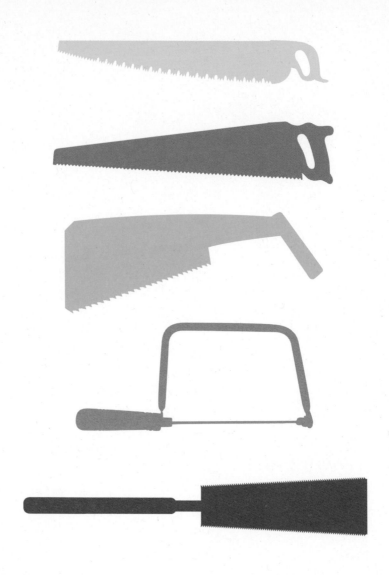

01 02 03 04 05

TOOL

01 02 03 04

TOOL

01 02 03 04 05

GARDENING

01 02 03 04

GARDENING

01 02 03 04

GARDENING

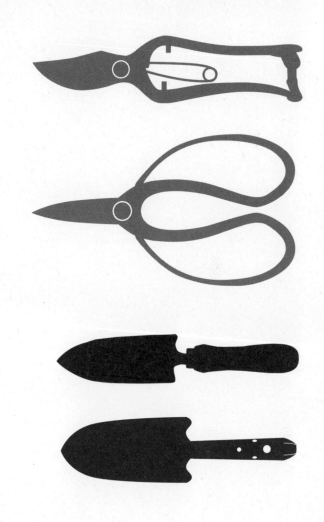

01 02 03 04

01 02 03 04 05

FLOWER

01 02 03 04 05 06

FLOWER

01 02 03 04

248

PLANT

01 02 03 04

PLANT

01 02 03 04 05

PLANT

01 02 03 04

PLANT

01

TREE

01 02 03

TREE 253

TREE

FREE STYLE SCRAPS 01
SILHOUETTE シルエット

2006 年 7 月 25 日	初版第 1 刷発行
2007 年 10 月 20 日	初版第 4 刷発行

編集・デザイン：	4D2A
イラスト：	荒井亮
	大川久志
	小熊未央
	坂上聡之 (METEOR)
	庄野祐輔
	佃弘樹
	古屋蔵人
	山森晋平
翻訳：	R.I.C. 出版株式会社
発行人：	籔内康一
発行所：	株式会社ビー・エヌ・エヌ新社
	〒 104-0042
	東京都中央区入船 3-7-2 35山京ビル
	Fax: 03-5543-3108
	Email: info@bnn.co.jp
印刷・製本：	株式会社 シナノ

©2006 4D2A
Printed in Japan
ISBN 4-86100-412-8